What if we do NOTHING?

OVERCROWDED WORLD

Ewan McLeish

W

FRANKLIN WATTS

LONDON • SYDNEY

First published in 2009 by Franklin Watts

© 2009 Arcturus Publishing Limited

Franklin Watts
338 Euston Road
London NW1 3BH

Franklin Watts Australia
Level 17/207 Kent Street, Sydney, NSW 2000

Produced by Arcturus Publishing Limited,
26/27 Bickels Yard, 151-153 Bermondsey Street,
London SE1 3HA

Series concept: Alex Woolf
Editor: Alex Woolf
Designer: Phipps Design
Picture researcher: Alex Woolf

The illustrations and diagrams on pages 7, 8, 9,
34 and 36 are by Phipps Design.

A CIP catalogue record for this book is available
from the British Library.

Dewey Decimal Classification Number: 363.9

ISBN 978 0 7496 8744 1

Printed in China

Franklin Watts is a division of Hachette
Children's Books, an Hachette Livre UK company.
www.hachettelivre.co.uk

Picture Credits
Corbis: 5 (Lynsey Addario), 11 (Wolfgang Langenstrassen/dpa),
13 (Rafiqur Rahman/Reuters), 14 (Bettmann), 19 (Tom Bean),
22 (Amit Dave/Reuters), 25 (Chris Hellier), 27 (Mimi Mollica),
28 (Mike F Alquinto/epa), 33 (Owen Franken),
37 (Jagadeesh/Reuters), 41 (Liz Gilbert/Sygma),
45 (Gideon Mendel).
Getty Images: 6 (George Marks/Stringer/Retrofile), 12 (NASA), 16
(John Moore/Staff), 21 (David Greedy/Stringer), 31 (AFP/Stringer),
35 (Yoshikazu Tsuno/Staff/AFP), 38 (Mychele Daniau/Staff/AFP),
42 (Mark Ralston/Staff/AFP).
Shutterstock: cover bottom left (Natalia Bratslavsky), cover top
right (Mario Bruno), cover background (gary718), 4 (Steve
Lovegrove).

Cover pictures
bottom left: Rush hour on an American freeway.
top right: A huge crowd of sports fans in Prague, Czech Republic.
background: The New York City midtown skyline at twilight.

Every attempt has been made to clear copyright. Should there be
any inadvertent omission, please apply to the publisher for
rectification.

Contents

CHAPTER 1

An Overcrowded World

It is the year 2025 and the world's population stands at nearly 8 billion. More parts of the world than ever before face serious food and water shortages. Famines are now commonplace events across much of Africa and Central Asia. In many towns, riots over food shortages disrupt everyday life. Continued environmental destruction and loss of productive land makes a bad situation worse. Meanwhile, oil and gas prices continue to rise as reserves run low and demand grows. Neither rich nor poor countries are spared these effects. In many places, housing is in short supply. Infrastructure (essential services such as public transportation and hospitals) can no longer meet demand. Cities have become overcrowded as millions of people move to them in search of better lives.

A realistic look into the future?

The world's current population stands at 6.7 billion people, nearly two and a half times what it was 50 years ago. Barring some major catastrophe, the population will continue to rise for years to come. Experts differ on precise numbers, but most agree that we will soon be living in an overcrowded world. Many would argue we already are.

Today, hunger and malnutrition kill nearly six million children a year, while many more live in poverty. The world is already showing signs of environmental damage and resources are stretched thin. The pressure on the land, sea and atmosphere to support our growing population is immense. Meanwhile, another 75 million people are added to the world's numbers every year.

Traffic jams like this are likely to become an increasingly common sight as the world population grows and the demand for transport rises.

Beyond the numbers

Rapid population growth will continue to threaten our ability to provide sufficient food and resources for all. The world will need as much food in the next 50 years as it consumed in the last 10,000! If overcrowding leads to environmental breakdown and human misery, then the situation can only get worse as the population grows.

The numbers don't tell the whole story, however. Many factors besides population can affect the well-being of a nation. The way resources are used, the way societies are organized and the way countries are governed are also important. This book will look at how different parts of the world have responded very differently to the challenge of overpopulation.

Afghan refugees fight for food at the Kili Faizo temporary camp on the Pakistan border. Sudden influxes of people, such as refugees, can destabilize countries, particularly in areas already experiencing rapid population growth.

DEBATE

You are in charge

You are the leader of a small but rich country with a stable population. A poorer, neighbouring country with a rapidly growing population asks for aid. Do you:

■ withhold that aid on the basis that the neighbouring country needs to become more self-sufficient?

■ negotiate an aid package that includes a commitment by the neighbouring country to address its population growth?

CHAPTER 2

A Growing Population

The year is 2025. China announced today that its population had reached 1.5 billion people. That is a lot of people, but the Chinese authorities were quick to emphasize what their massive country had achieved in limiting population growth. Western experts agree that China's birth rate is lower than that of many other countries. However, they point out that there is likely to be a rise in the birth rate in the next few years as China begins to encourage couples to have more children instead of fewer. The change in policy is because China no longer has enough young people to support its rapidly ageing population. Meanwhile, India is fast catching up with its giant neighbour. Most predictions suggest that India will overtake China's population by the year 2040.

A growth spurt

Throughout most of history, the growth of the human population has been slow and uneven. Tens of thousands of years passed before our species reached the one billion mark – in around the year 1800. It took only 130 more years to add the next billion and another 33 years to reach 3 billion. Just 36 years later, the population had doubled to reach six billion by 1999. By 2008, we were more than half way to the next billion (forecast for 2013). All current estimates suggest we will reach eight billion by 2028 and nine billion roughly halfway through this century.

This picture of a quiet Manhattan street was taken in the 1950s when the population of the United States was 150 million. Since that time it has doubled in number.

The chart below shows the dramatic growth in the world's population, particularly since 1950. However, the chart also shows that the number of people added to the population each year – the population increment – actually reached a peak in the 1980s and 1990s. Since then, that number has been declining. In 1970, world population growth was around 2 per cent per year; now it is 1.1 per cent.

For the world as a whole, the rate of increase in population, in percentage terms, has been declining for several decades. However, the number of extra people added to the world's population every year is still very high indeed (between 70 and 80 million in the early 2000s, as the chart shows).

POPULATION GROWTH

This chart shows overall population growth since 1750. It also shows the population increment. That is the number of people added to the world's population each year (averaged over each decade) since that date. The chart includes forecasts until 2050.

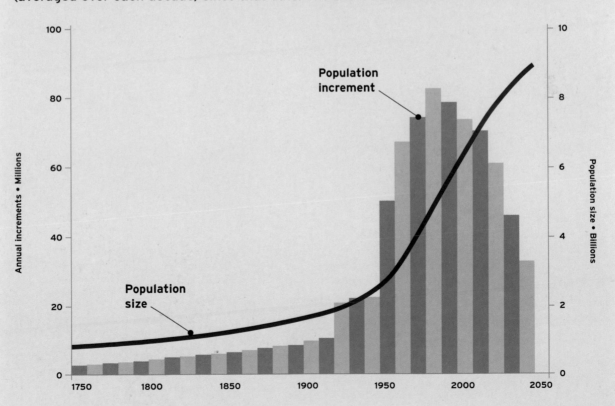

Source: www.eoearth.org/article/Human_population-explosion

Where people live

Of course, six billion people sounds like a lot! But what does it really mean? Are we really living in an overcrowded world? It is sometimes possible to travel for kilometres without seeing much sign of human habitation. But there are also massive, sprawling cities with 10 or 15 or even 20 million people crammed into high-rise blocks or squalid shantytowns. Clearly, people are not spread evenly across the face of the earth. Different countries and regions support dramatically different numbers of people.

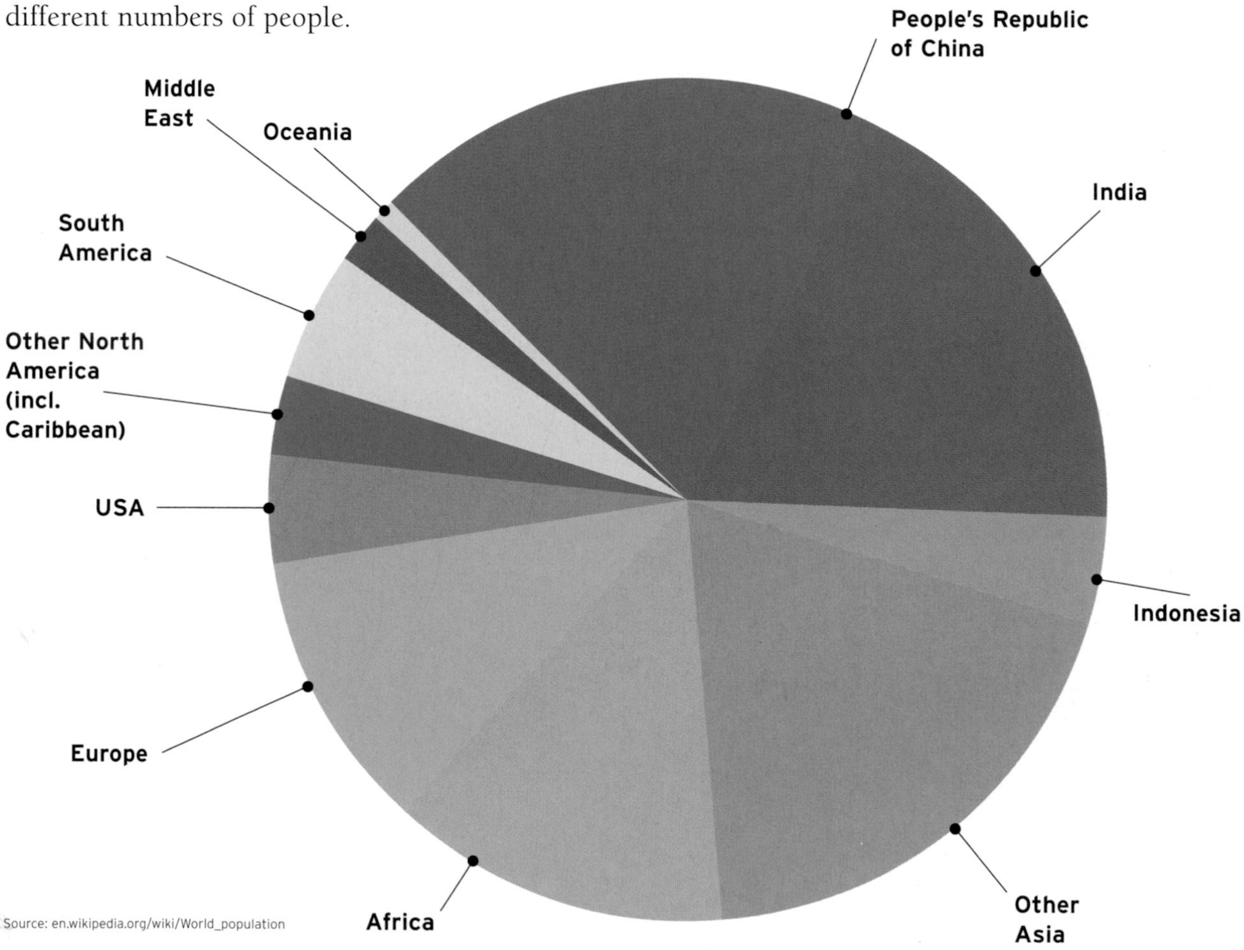

People's Republic of China

India

Indonesia

Other Asia

Africa

Europe

USA

Other North America (incl. Caribbean)

South America

Middle East

Oceania

Source: en.wikipedia.org/wiki/World_population

The pie chart on this page shows the distribution of the world population by country, continent or region. Perhaps the most notable feature of the chart is that two countries, China and India, make up 37 per cent of the world's population, while Asia as a whole makes up over 60 per cent. Two other continents, Europe and Africa, contribute a further 11 per cent and 12 per cent respectively. North America adds another 8 per cent and South America 5.3 per cent.

This pie chart shows that China makes the single largest contribution to the world's population, as great as the whole of North America and Europe put together.

8

The table on this page lists the ten most populated countries. These countries differ greatly in size, so population figures on their own do not tell us a great deal about how populations are distributed.

Still rising – but not as fast

The highest rate of population growth (2.04 per cent per year) occurred in the late 1960s. Since then the rate of population growth has been declining, although not fast enough to stop the actual numbers continuing to rise for the next two decades (see page 7). Today, the actual number of people added to the population each year is beginning to decrease. Most estimates suggest that the overall population will finally peak towards the end of this century. By then it may be 10 or 11 billion.

THE TEN MOST POPULATED COUNTRIES

Country	Population	% world population
China	1.32 billion	20%
India	1.12 billion	17%
United States	300 million	4.6%
Indonesia	225 million	3.5%
Brazil	186 million	2.8%
Pakistan	158 million	2.5%
Bangladesh	147 million	2.3%
Russia	143 million	2.2%
Nigeria	140 million	2.1%
Japan	128 million	2.0%

GLOBAL POPULATION DENSITY

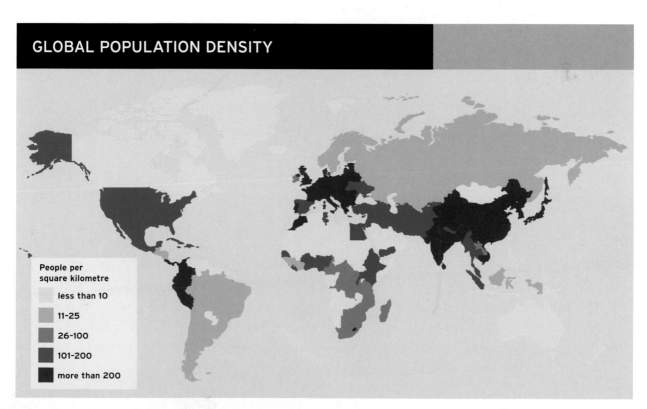

People per square kilometre

- less than 10
- 11-25
- 26-100
- 101-200
- more than 200

Poor and overpopulated

Although the world's population is still growing rapidly, it is important to understand that this growth is not evenly distributed around the world. Of the 75 million people added each year, 95 per cent live in the less developed or poorer regions of the world, particularly Africa and South-East Asia. These are often the regions least able to cope with increases in their populations. The table on the right shows the nine countries that are predicted to make the greatest contribution to the world's population over the next 40 years – well over 50 per cent of the increase, in fact.

Losing ground?

At the other end of the scale, many parts of the world show a much slower or stable rate of increase. Some regions are actually experiencing a population decline. These tend to be the richer parts of the world. Falling populations can also be found in places where war or disease (particularly AIDS) has increased mortality (death) rates, such as parts of Southern Africa. Population decline can also occur in places with poor economies or unhealthy environments. This has happened in parts of Eastern Europe and Central Asia.

HIGHEST PROJECTED POPULATION GROWTH RATES

Country	Addition to world population
India	580 million
Nigeria	154 million
Pakistan	135 million
Democratic Republic of Congo	130 million
Bangladesh	104 million
Uganda	103 million
USA	100 million
Ethiopia	87 million
China	80 million

NIGERIA: A GROWING PROBLEM?

Nigeria is the most highly populated country in Africa. A census (population count) taken in 2006 gave the population as 140 million. By 2050 the population is predicted to be 289 million. According to the United Nations, Nigeria is currently experiencing a population explosion, with one of the highest fertility rates in the world. Health care and general living conditions in Nigeria are poor. Life expectancy is 47 years, and only half the population has access to clean water and adequate sanitation.

This young Nigerian mother waits with two of her children at a health clinic. The fertility rate in Nigeria in 2008 was approximately 5.41 children per woman, compared to 2.1 in the United States and 1.85 in the United Kingdom.

DEBATE

You are in charge

You are a United Nations official who has been asked to predict the population growth of a certain developing country. What kind of data, do you think, will be most helpful to you?

- birth and death rates
- life expectancy
- the percentage of children going to primary school.

What other information might you ask for in order to help you with your prediction?

Thomas Malthus (1766-1834) predicted that, as population increased, the world would run out of food. This has not yet happened but food shortages are common in many parts of the world.

Malthus was not entirely correct in his predictions. He had not allowed for the effect the industrial and agricultural revolutions of the 18th and 19th centuries would have on the supply of resources. In fact, world food production has actually outstripped human population growth. This does not mean, however, that food is evenly distributed or that people in all parts of the world have enough to eat.

For species other than humans, overpopulation is sometimes described as a situation in which a species' numbers exceed the capacity (ability) of its environment to support it in terms of food and shelter. In the case of humans, however, most people would also consider 'quality of life' in addition to the bare necessities of life.

Quality of life includes adequate employment, recreational space, medical care, education, transportation, clean air and freedom from crime. These things also require and use up resources.

Overpopulation in human terms cannot simply be defined in terms of numbers of people or the availability of resources. Overpopulation can be described as a situation in which the population density in a particular place is so great that it reduces the quality of life, damages the environment and leads to shortages of essential goods and services.

THE DISAPPEARING PEOPLE

Rapa Nui (or Easter Island) is a tiny island of 170 square kilometres in the middle of the Pacific Ocean. Between 1000 AD and 1650 its population increased rapidly to a density of over 100 people per square kilometre (20,000 people). Yet, by the time the Dutch explorer Jacob Roggeveen arrived there in 1722, the fertile, tree-covered island was bare and the people in decline. By the end of the 19th century the population was 132. No one can say for sure what befell the people of Rapa Nui. However, one explanation is that the island simply became overpopulated. Their decline was due to overuse of the island's resources, leading to deforestation, erosion of the soil and the loss of wood for fuel and boat building. Without boats, the people could no longer sustain themselves by fishing.

The causes of overpopulation

There may be many reasons for overpopulation. The most obvious is an increase in the birth rate. This may be for a particular reason. For example, after the end of the Second World War, there was a sharp rise in birth rates (known as 'the baby boom') in Europe, Asia, North America and Australia as families were reunited and the threat of death or injury subsided. There may be cultural or religious reasons for high birth rates. There may also be purely practical or economic reasons for people wanting large families.

Riviona, seven, pauses in the small field of corn that feeds her family in central Zimbabwe. With the destruction of Zimbabwe's farming system by Robert Mugabe, many people rely on these small plots to feed themselves.

Overpopulation isn't only caused by high birth rates. Medical advances and better health care have reduced mortality rates, so more people are surviving infancy and people are also living longer. Migration can also cause a particular region to become overpopulated as large numbers of people move from one country or region to another.

Overpopulation may also occur for reasons that have nothing to do with population growth. Natural disasters, conflict and poor government can lead to situations in which available resources can no longer support a population. Zimbabwe, for example, was once known as 'the breadbasket of southern Africa'. Despite periodic droughts, farmers in Zimbabwe grew enough food to both feed the country and export food to surrounding nations. In 2000, the president,

FOR RICHER, FOR POORER

Countries undergoing rapid population growth are often the ones that seem to struggle the most with poverty and environmental problems. Ethiopia, for example, has more fertile land per person than the United Kingdom and a low population density of 70 people per square kilometre. Its population, however, has grown from 18 million in 1950 to 77 million today. By 2050 it is expected to reach 170 million. Now, a combination of droughts, poor government, high population growth, inefficient agriculture, internal conflict, poor infrastructure and widespread poverty have meant that famines are a regular occurrence in many parts of the country.

Robert Mugabe, began evicting farmers and bringing farmland under state control. As a result, the farms were poorly managed or abandoned. Vital irrigation equipment was no longer maintained or was simply vandalized or looted for scrap. By early 2008, six to seven million people in Zimbabwe were threatened with famine. Yet Zimbabwe has one of the lowest population densities in the whole of Africa, around 33 per square kilometre.

Living beyond our means

So, overpopulation can be caused not only by population growth but also by a reduction in available resources. Scarcity of resources can be caused by different factors within particular countries, but in a more general sense we are all responsible. People the world over are living beyond the capacity of the planet to support their way of life. However, not everyone is consuming resources at the same pace. People, particularly in Europe and North America, continue to use up resources at an unparalleled rate. To raise everyone's living standards to the levels enjoyed in richer countries would require the resources of another two or three entire planets. That is clearly not an option. We must therefore look at other ways of meeting our needs in a sustainable way.

DEBATE

You are in charge

You have recently been elected prime minister of a developing country. You campaigned on a platform of agricultural reform, including making more land available to farmers. You are under pressure from the opposition party to deliver on your promises. Meanwhile, a severe drought is forecast. Do you:

- implement your reforms as quickly as possible, even though you know it will take time for the new arrangements to work properly?

- delay the reforms and concentrate on short-term measures, such as building more storage facilities to stave off the worst effects of the famine?

CHAPTER 4

The Impact of Overpopulation

The year is 2025 and for the third night in a row, riots over the lack of water are being reported from all over the cities of Los Angeles and Las Vegas. Local authorities imposed a ban on all uses of water except for drinking, cooking and essential washing needs. Some parts of these densely populated cities have running water for only a few hours a day. Poorer areas get none at all. The rioters say the problem has been getting worse for decades. They blame the government for lack of planning.

Even today, people disagree over whether we have reached, or gone beyond, the limits of our global resources. Some take the view that the impact of overpopulation on our environment is now so severe that the damage to land, water and the atmosphere is irreversible. Others believe that, with better management, there are still enough resources to support further population growth. So what is the evidence that overpopulation has had an impact on resources – and what will happen if we do nothing?

Improvements in farming methods and increased mechanization during the 19th and early 20th centuries enabled food production to keep pace with a growing world population. Later in the 20th century, scientists developed vastly improved strains of wheat, maize and rice, as well as powerful new fertilizers and pesticides, many of them obtained from fossil fuels. This led to a new agricultural revolution, sometimes called the Green Revolution. Crop yields increased by up to ten times.

These advances came at a cost. Many developing countries switched the focus of their agriculture from traditional, small-scale farming to the mass production of

THE FIGHT FOR FOOD

'The world is richer today than it was ten years ago. There is more food available and still more could be produced.... The knowledge and resources to reduce hunger are there. What is lacking is sufficient political will to mobilize those resources to the benefit of the hungry.'

Food and Agriculture Organization (part of the United Nations), 2006

just a few varieties of crops. These crops were often more suitable for export (cash crops, such as tea, coffee and palm oil) than local consumption. Local people lost their farms to large multinational food-producing companies. While the exports brought much-needed revenue to the countries concerned, the losers were often local people who had depended on their small plots for survival.

Harvesting grain in North Dakota, USA. Vast farms like this can produce enormous quantities of food but the price of grain and problems of distribution worldwide mean that it will not be available to everyone.

At the same time, the use of chemical fertilizers and pesticides often had damaging, sometimes devastating, effects on the environment. The natural nutrient cycles, in which land was allowed to stay uncultivated for periods of time in order to recover, no longer occurred. Fertile soil turned to dust and blew away, a process known as desertification. Single crops, often unsuited to local conditions, were more vulnerable to disease and drought. If they failed, there was nothing to replace them.

And what of the future? Will there be another Green Revolution? Can food production rates continue rising to match the population? If so, it is likely to come about, at least in part, through genetic engineering. Scientists are already developing new varieties of crops, genetically modified to withstand saline (salty) or dry conditions. Similarly, staple crops, such as rice, are being engineered to contain higher levels of vitamins and protein. Better storage facilities and methods of distribution could also improve food supply.

However, even these developments are unlikely to satisfy demand. Hunger and malnutrition continue to kill nearly six million children every year, and the situation is getting worse. More people were malnourished in Sub-Saharan Africa in 2008 than in 1998.

NIGERIA

Nigeria is a country about the size of Texas. It is losing about 3,500 square kilometres of crop and grazing land to desertification every year. Over 35 million people are affected by this loss of fertile land. Meanwhile, Nigeria's livestock population (sheep, cattle and goats) has expanded 10 times since 1960. Now, people and animals compete for the same land, while Nigeria's rapidly growing population is being squeezed into an ever-smaller area.

Land under pressure

A growing population needs more land, not just to live on, but to produce food. Today, more than 25 per cent of the world's total land area has been given over to growing crops or raising livestock. This includes a third of all temperate (non-tropical) and tropical forests and a quarter of natural grasslands. Of course, people use land for many other purposes as well. Hydroelectric dams, urban development, mining and timber extraction all consume land. As the population rises, the process of converting natural areas for human purposes will inevitably continue.

At the same time, population growth is also causing a reduction in usable land. Over-cultivated land is frequently lost to desertification. Also, over-extraction of water has made large areas of land less useful because of salinization (increased salt levels). Salinization occurs because when surface soils dry out, salt-laden water, deeper in the water table, is drawn to the surface.

A scientist inspects a genetically modified rice plant at a research station in the Philippines. Research into improved strains of staple foods continues, but this work is unlikely to keep pace with population increases.

In the future, land is also likely to be lost as a result of global warming. Since the mid-20th century, global temperatures have risen. Most scientists believe this is caused by increasing levels of carbon dioxide and other 'greenhouse gases' that trap heat in the atmosphere. Much of this increase is a result of human activity, notably the burning of fossil fuels. Global warming is likely to cause a rise in sea levels and increased flooding. This will tend to affect the most productive agricultural areas, since they are often low lying or in flood plains.

People gather to draw water from a huge well in the village of Natwarghad, Gujarat. Dams, wells and ponds frequently run dry in this part of western India, forcing people to wait for hours around ponds for state-run water tankers to arrive.

Water, water everywhere?

Although the water supply is constantly replenished through the water cycle, we are now using it far faster than it is being replaced. Water tables (underground water levels) are currently falling in large countries, including China, the United States and India, as well as in many smaller countries, such as Pakistan, Iran, Algeria and Mexico. In some countries, such as China, this is already leading to shortages of grain. Experts predict that an extra 1.3 billion people will be added to the world's population by 2025 and most of them will be born in countries already experiencing water shortages.

WATER FROM THE SEA

Malta obtains two-thirds of its fresh water from seawater through a process called desalination, which removes salt from the water. The process of desalination often requires large amounts of energy. It is also costly to transport the water to areas far from the sea, making this an expensive and wasteful technology. A 2004 report by the University of Hamburg points out, 'Desalinated water may be the solution for some regions, but not for places that are poor, deep in the interior of a continent, or at high elevation. Unfortunately, that includes some of the places with the greatest water problems.' In May 2008 London's new mayor approved the construction of a 140 million litre a day desalination plant in the Thames Estuary.

Running on empty?

You might be surprised to learn that the countries with the largest populations don't consume the most energy resources. With only five per cent of the world's population, the United States consumes more than a quarter (26 per cent) of the world's total energy, 80 per cent of which is from fossil fuels. Europe, with 11 per cent of the world's population, follows with 22 per cent of world energy use. China, with a massive 20 per cent of the population, still only uses 15.5 per cent of the world's energy.

These figures demonstrate that a country or region's level of economic development, more than the size of its population, dictates how much energy it uses. The rapid industrialization of China, India and other developing countries is more likely to increase the demand for energy than a rise in population will.

A declining environment

Throughout history, human populations have shaped and altered the natural environment. As the population has risen, the impact on the environment has increased. Since 1900, that impact has been global. Activities such as food production, construction, mining and transport have led, for example, to the increasingly rapid loss of forests, pollution of the world's oceans, declining fish stocks and global warming. Meanwhile, the development of modern technologies, such as the petrol and diesel engine, explosives, modern agricultural machinery and even the chain saw, has increased our capacity to change – and damage – our surroundings.

Frequently, the most serious cases of environmental damage occur in poor countries. Poor people do not deliberately set out to wreck their own environments, but simply lack the means to protect them adequately. Often it is the rich nations, with their enormous demand for natural resources, which drive the destruction. Japan, for example, is a highly populated country but relatively poor in resources. It is responsible for much of the logging that is causing large-scale deforestation in South-East Asia. One effect of this exploitation by richer nations is that it often deprives poorer countries of the land and resources they need to support their own rapidly growing populations.

MADAGASCAR

The Indian Ocean island of Madagascar has a population of nearly 19 million but a population density of only 32 people per square kilometre. It has, however, one of the fastest-growing populations in the world. A combination of rapid population growth and poor management has led to over-exploitation of the island's resources, especially its forests. Madagascar has lost nearly 90 per cent of its forests through logging and forest clearance for farmland. The island's water resources have also been negatively affected. In July 2007, the United Nations listed six rainforest parks in Madagascar as World Heritage sites. This will give protection to a few remaining areas, while permitting some use of resources by local people.

This is a recently deforested area in Madagascar. Farmers burn large areas of forest each year to clear land for crops. Deforestation is threatening many of Madagascar's plant and animal species.

Migration

It is natural for people to want to improve their chances of having a good and reasonably prosperous life, both for themselves and for their families. Many are denied that possibility because of poverty and lack of resources.

Not surprisingly, the majority of these people live in developing countries and look to the richer parts of the world for new opportunities. The United Nations predicts that between 2005 and 2050 the net increase in migrants to developed regions (that is the difference between the number entering and the number leaving) will be around 98 million.

People often migrate to another country because of the effects of overpopulation, including scarcity of food, water and shelter, and poor quality of life. But overpopulation is not the only reason – civil wars, persecution and natural disasters also force people from their homeland. Even so, it is likely that, as populations in poorer countries increase, the pressure to find a better life elsewhere will too.

A LONG JOURNEY

'Twenty-five migrants last night were missing, believed dead, in the Mediterranean after a rescue attempt went tragically wrong. The migrants were among 28 people on a small open boat, which was intercepted by a Greek tug, 72 miles south of Malta. As the tug approached, the migrants moved to one side and the boat capsized. Maltese officials said migrant flows across the Mediterranean had increased since patrols by the EU's [European Union] border control agency ended this month.'

The *Guardian*, August 2007

Migration can bring benefits and problems to both the countries that migrants leave and the countries they enter. Migrants bring new ideas, tax revenue (income), new skills and, usually, the will to work hard. They may also put more pressure on housing, infrastructure and other resources in the host country. Large-scale migrations, in

A vessel containing over 300 immigrants from Eritrea is spotted by an Italian Customs Police helicopter. Most will be sent back to their own country. Every year, thousands of immigrants try to reach Europe. Some die in the attempt.

particular, can create tensions between immigrants and the local community. This is especially so when the local community does not offer immigrants support to help them to integrate, or when immigrant communities prefer to keep themselves separate. Meanwhile, the countries they leave may lose people with valuable skills. Well-qualified people – doctors, engineers and nurses, for example – are more likely to be welcomed elsewhere.

The rise and rise of the city

Lack of opportunity and jobs in rural areas, and the promise of employment, housing and greater security, have encouraged the movement of people into towns and cities worldwide. In 1800, only 3 per cent of people lived in cities. By the end of the 20th century, that figure had risen to 50 per cent. If these trends continue, by 2030 city dwellers will comprise 60 per cent of the world's population, or nearly five billion people.

Many will not enjoy a comfortable life, however. Around two billion will be crowded into so-called shantytowns – makeshift and ramshackle developments at the edges of cities. Shantytowns lack basic sanitation and health care and suffer high crime rates. A lack of education and opportunity creates a cycle of poverty.

The rise of cities will be most keenly felt in the developing world, where most population growth is occurring. In Africa and Asia, for example, the urban population is set to double by 2030.

The impact of these cities, not only on the poor themselves, but also on the wider environment, is hard to predict. Such rapid growth requires planning, investment in infrastructure and social support. Without these things, many cities may become engulfed in violence, crime and poverty. Even so, as the United Nations states, 'Cities concentrate poverty, but they also represent the best hope of

A shantytown in the city of Manila, Philippines. A recent report by the UN states that more than 10 million Filipinos have no access to safe drinking water, and more than 21 million lack basic sanitation.

escaping it'. Most countries become more urbanized as they develop. The challenge is to manage this development while catering to the needs of a rapidly growing population.

GOING URBAN

'By 2030, the towns and cities of the developing world will make up 81 per cent of urban humanity.'

State of the World Population 2007, United Nations Population Fund

A growing threat

Overpopulation uses up resources, including productive land. As the population grows, these pressures can only intensify. More people will suffer shortages of the basic essentials of life, such as food and housing. The United Nations suggests that about 850 million people are currently malnourished or starving, and a staggering 1.1 billion do not have access to safe drinking water. Often linked to this extreme poverty are high levels of infant and child mortality, high crime rates and low life expectancy.

Poverty

Interestingly, poverty levels are not rising as quickly as the world population is growing. In fact there is evidence to show that, worldwide, the percentage of people in poverty (defined as people who live on less than one US dollar per day) is actually shrinking as the population grows. The World Bank reports that in 1990, 29 per cent of the global population lived in poverty. In 2008, that figure had dropped to less than 18 per cent. This decrease is because the world experienced strong economic growth during that period. Poor countries have become wealthier, due to support from richer nations and international agencies such as the World Bank.

Poverty as a *percentage* of the global population may be declining but as the world population grows, the total *number* of poor people remains very high, and in some parts of the world it is increasing. For example, due to Africa's high population growth, the absolute number of Africans living at or below the US$1 a day level, is still rising.

Endangered species

Poverty and hunger are not the only consequences of rising populations. As more land, particularly forest, is used for food production and other human activities, the pressure on habitats, and therefore on other species, also increases. This is especially true of large mammals. Elephants, big cats and great apes such as orang-utans and gorillas are all under threat.

This elephant has been killed in a head-on collision with a train in north-eastern India. Wild elephants have been moving out of the jungles as people move into forested areas.

A BLEAK PICTURE

'Clearly the past half century has been a traumatic (painful) one, as the combined impact of human numbers, consumption per individual, and our choice of technology continue to exploit rapidly an increasing proportion of the world's resources at an unsustainable rate. During a remarkably short period of time, we have lost a quarter of the world's topsoil and a fifth of its agricultural land, altered the composition of the atmosphere profoundly, and destroyed a major proportion of our forests and other natural habitats without replacing them. Worst of all, we have driven the rate of biological extinction, the permanent loss of species, up several hundred times ... and are threatened with the loss of a majority of all species by the end of the 21st century.'

American Association for the Advancement of Science, Atlas of Population and Environment

Other threats

Overpopulation, and the resulting pressure on scarce resources such as fertile land, oil and water, may have other impacts, including:

- increased levels of pollution as cities become more crowded
- the outbreak of epidemics as people are forced to live in overcrowded, unhygienic conditions
- high crime rates and the breakdown of families
- war and conflict

DEBATE

You are in charge

You are in charge of immigration policy for your country. Millions of illegal immigrants are already working in your country and thousands more are entering illegally every day. Do you focus on:

■ increasing border security to make it harder for illegal immigrants to enter the country?

■ rounding up illegal immigrants to send them back to their home countries?

■ allowing those already working in your country to gain legal status to integrate them into society?

CHAPTER 5

Changing Populations

The year is 2025. At Hyogo Retirement Home, Osaka, Japan, a young journalist interviews Akiko Tanaka, an 85-year-old resident. 'I am happy here,' says Tanaka, 'but I worry for our country. When I was a young man, Japan was still recovering from World War II. Everyone seemed young then, and full of hope. Now everyone seems old. Perhaps it is living here that makes me see things this way. But even when I look at the passers-by from my window I seem to see only the elderly. How will we survive as a nation? Where are the young? Where are they?'

The average age of Japan's population has been increasing for some time. The same is true for most of the world's richer nations. Populations are changing everywhere. But why is it happening and why should it matter?

Back to basics

While the world's population is rising overall, some regions are experiencing greater increases than others, and in some countries populations are even declining. We have also seen that the rate of growth of the world's population, though still fast, is actually slowing.

In 2006, the United Nations produced an important report on the state of the world's population. It made the following observations:

- Almost all population growth will take place in the less developed regions, notably Africa and Asia. By contrast, the population of the more developed regions will remain mostly unchanged.
- In the 1950s, the average number of children born per woman, worldwide, was about five. Now it is 2.56. This is expected to decline further to 2.05 by 2050. This means the growth rate has fallen from 2 per cent per year at its peak to 1.3 per cent in 2006.
- In developing countries, the fertility rate is about three children

per woman (down from six in 1950). In the more developed regions, it is frequently below two per woman – less than the rate of about 2.1 that is needed to replace the parent generation and keep a population stable.

■ At the same time, life expectancy overall (with some exceptions) has risen from 56 to 65 years. In 2050, it will be 76. This means that the population as a whole is ageing, particularly in the developed world.

Elderly people take part in an exercise routine in a retirement home in Minneapolis, Minnesota, USA. Better care means that people are living longer but this also means that the average age of many populations is increasing.

Rising or falling?

Birth rates are declining in both the developing and developed regions of the world. However, the greatest decline is in the richer countries. As pointed out by the UN, the fertility rate is now below the rate needed to keep the population stable (2.1 children per woman). In Italy, for example, it is as low as 1.26!

A trend has become apparent. As countries develop and become wealthier, they tend to undergo a 'demographic transition' – a change from one population state to another. This is marked by both falling birth rates and falling death rates. The population stays the same or drops, but there are more older people than younger.

Four steps to a stable population

How does the demographic transition happen? In the early stages of a country's development, both birth and death rates are high and there is little sustained growth in the population (stage 1 in the diagram below). Later on, advances in technology and medicine and improved health and welfare cause death rates to fall. Birth rates remain high and population growth rates begin to soar (stage 2).

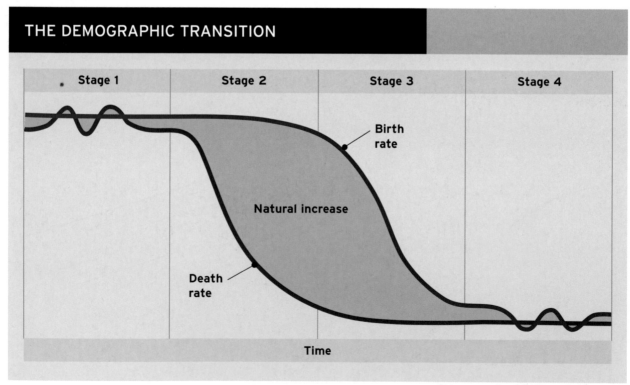

THE DEMOGRAPHIC TRANSITION

Stage 1 Stage 2 Stage 3 Stage 4

Birth rate

Natural increase

Death rate

Time

Source: www.eoearth.org/article/Human_population_explosion

Then, after some decades of declining death rates, families in those countries develop both the desire and the means to limit birth rates (stage 3). Birth rates fall, often rapidly, to approach the low death rates, and population growth slows or even goes into reverse (stage 4).

TOP HEAVY WORLD?

People who study population trends predict that by 2050 the number of people in the world over the age of 60 will more than triple from about 600 million now to nearly 1.9 billion. That is more than 20 per cent of the world's population. In countries with declining populations, the over-60s could comprise as much as 30 to 40 per cent.

A number of factors may explain these changes. For example, as living standards rise, education and career opportunities improve, particularly for women. Many marry later and have smaller families in order to devote more time to their careers. In some countries, such as Italy, the high cost of living and the lack of affordable childcare are additional reasons to have smaller families.

Also, as a country develops, the economic advantages of having children begin to disappear. In many poor and rural economies, children are an important part of the workforce and are also seen as a support in old age. As families become more financially secure, and societies more industrialized, there is less need to have large numbers of children and so the birth rate drops.

A Japanese working mother picks up her daughter from a nursery room or 'Kangaroom' run by her employer, a cosmetics firm. The desire or need for both parents to work is one reason why Japan's fertility rate is only 1.3.

Age matters

Although the demographic transition helps to reduce the problem of overpopulation, it also creates its own difficulties. As birth rates decline, the age profile of a population changes and the average age rises. This can be seen when one looks at the age profile of a developed country such as France. By contrast, a developing country like India, which has yet to experience a demographic transition, has a very different age profile.

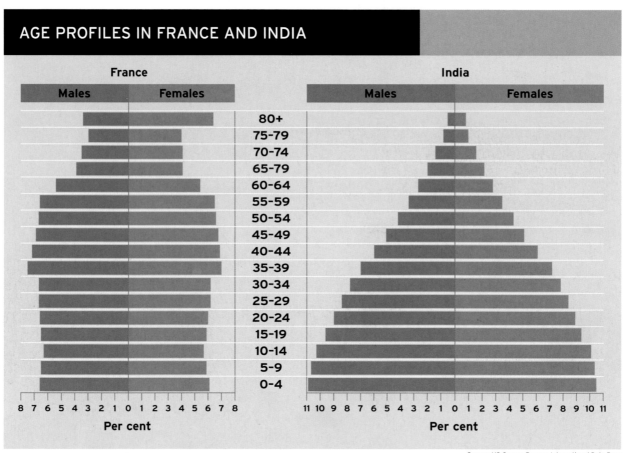

AGE PROFILES IN FRANCE AND INDIA

Source: US Census Bureau, International Data Base

In the diagrams above, the differences are immediately apparent. India's age profile is shaped like a triangle, while France's has a narrower shape. In India, over 30 per cent of the population are children under 15 years old. They will replace the generations above them and provide the workforce to drive India's economy and support its old people in years to come. In France, as in much of the Western world, fewer children may mean that the economy starts to slow down and economic stagnation occurs. As the population ages and people live longer, there will be greater pressure on social and health care services. With fewer people entering the workforce, tax revenues will fall, leaving governments with less money to support those services. A declining workforce will also make a smaller contribution to the pensions of a rapidly growing retired population. Immigration from the developing to the developed countries may be one way in which the effects of this economic slowdown can be addressed.

Different stages

Each part of the world is at a different stage of the demographic transition. Birth rates in most countries in Africa, Asia and Latin America are well above the replacement rate (2.1 children per woman) required to keep their populations stable. In some countries, the proportion of people under the age of 15 can be as high as 45 to 50 per cent. With such a high proportion of young people, even if birth rates fall to replacement levels, it will take 70 years – an average person's lifetime – before population growth ends. The United States is the exception among developed nations. With a birth rate of 2.09 and a high rate of immigration, its population is still growing rapidly (1 per cent per year), suggesting a population increase of 42 per cent by 2050.

This call centre in Bangalore, India, provides cheap customer service helplines for companies around the world. This helps the economies of developing countries, like India, but may threaten jobs in countries where the businesses are based.

A demographic timebomb?

How will different parts of the world cope with declining numbers of young people and an ageing population? Some solutions to these problems are already becoming apparent. For example, as workforces in the richer countries decline, some jobs will be moved, or 'outsourced', to developing countries such as India, where there is an increasingly skilled (and youthful) workforce. This process will

PLUGGING THE GAP

In 2008, the US utility industry calculated that the retirement of its ageing workforce would produce key job shortages in the following few years. It began a scheme of career extension and 'geezer-retention' policies to address these needs.

Experience counts. These two French mechanics are over 70. France is attempting to adapt to an older population by employing more older people. Currently many French people retire or become unemployed between 55 and 64.

help these countries develop more rapidly, speeding up their own demographic transitions. Planned migration can also meet the needs of developed countries for skilled and less skilled labour. At the same time, migration can reduce some of the pressures of overpopulation on developing countries.

There may also be unexpected benefits to the demographic transition. Falling birth rates mean that fewer resources will be needed to support and educate the young. Crime rates are also likely to fall as living standards rise. A non-growing population will place less pressure on a nation's infrastructure – roads, railways, housing, schools, hospitals, power plants and the like.

But with a smaller workforce, governments may not receive enough in tax to pay the pensions of a large retired population. Governments may have to encourage people to retire later. People are, after all, living longer and retaining their health and vigour far beyond the traditional retirement age of 60 or 65. The expertise and experience of older people is being increasingly recognized, with many businesses retaining their older staff, at least on a part-time basis. Working longer means people will continue to pay into pension funds and will collect pensions for fewer years when they do retire. That, in turn, makes more money available for the growing number of retirees who depend on pensions.

DEBATE

You are in charge

You are a politician in the ruling party in India. You understand the significance of the demographic transition but are concerned that any population changes will occur too slowly to save your country from the effects of overpopulation. Do you:

- try to speed up the transition with an intensive media campaign and financial incentives to encourage people to have smaller families?
- recognize that the transition cannot be forced and concentrate instead on improving living standards?

CHAPTER 6

A Way Forward

The year is 2025. It is nearly 20 years since the United Nations produced its 2006 report on population. Now it is about to publish another report, 20 Years On. The report will show that many of its 2006 predictions have come true. The world population stands at just below eight billion, as the report forecast. But some evidence suggests growth rates are falling faster than predicted. With help from richer nations, some developing countries have begun to address problems such as poverty and desertification. With greater investment in education and health care, living standards have risen. As their long-term economic security improves, families are opting to have fewer children. A UN spokesperson said, 'We still have a long way to go, but the signs are encouraging. Perhaps the world is finally getting to grips with the problem of overpopulation.'

A better future?

Generally speaking, population growth rates decline as societies develop. However, the change doesn't happen quickly and many experts argue that the rate of population growth in much of the world is already unsustainable.

Some countries have tried more direct approaches to the problem of overpopulation. In the 1980s, the government of Bangladesh invited foreign aid workers to educate people about birth control and family planning. As a result the fertility rate halved from 6.2 in the 1970s to 3.1 in the 2000s. Many countries have sought to limit the flow of immigrants across their borders by applying strict rules for entry. However, one of the most radical and far-reaching approaches to the issue of overpopulation was undertaken by China some 30 years ago.

China's One-Child Policy

In 1979, the new leader of China, Deng Xiaoping, aimed to slow the country's rapidly rising population. He launched a national

programme of birth control called the One-Child Policy. The government pressured couples to have only one child, especially in urban areas. In rural areas, families were allowed to have two children, but only if the first child was female or disabled. Large fines were imposed on families who had additional children.

In many ways, the programme achieved its aims. The fertility rate in China dropped from more than five births to just 1.7 births per woman, well below the replacement rate. By 2008, the government estimated that the country had three or four hundred million fewer people than it would have had if the One-Child Policy had not been introduced.

A woman receives family planning advice in Ivory Coast, West Africa. Better access to services like these means that parents can plan their families and are less likely to have large numbers of children.

The policy had some unforeseen social consequences. Traditional Chinese families (like those of many other societies) tend to value boys above girls, because they consider them more capable of supporting the family economically. Some girl children were killed or abandoned and China began to develop a 'boy-heavy' population. In 2000, the gender ratio at birth in China was 117 boys to 100 girls. The only children became known as 'little emperors', because they were overindulged by their doting parents. This lack of balance led to health and social problems.

As the One-Child Policy enters its third generation, many people believe it has been too successful. One young adult now generally supports two parents and four grandparents. At the same time, China has undergone a demographic transition. Improvements in education and the economy have caused more couples to want fewer

Chinese parents pose for a photograph with their son. China's One-Child Policy has reduced population growth but led to other problems. As China's economy improves, however, richer couples are likely to risk fines by having more children.

children anyway. Many in China are concerned about a future in which a smaller workforce will have to support an ageing population. However, in March 2008, the Chinese government announced that the policy would remain in place for at least another decade.

China's experience suggests that forcing people to have fewer children is unpopular and difficult to put into practice. Many would also argue that it is morally wrong.

The ideal population

Many people argue that the world is overcrowded, but what might an uncrowded world be like? Is there an ideal population level? Keep in mind that the present level (6.7 billion people) is only possible because a large proportion of the population has access to only a few of the world's resources. Any estimate of an ideal population must take into account a future in which many more people have a reasonable standard of living.

A 1996 study by the University of Stanford in the United States suggests that the ideal world population is around two billion. This would allow a fairer distribution of wealth without putting excessive pressure on the world's resources. Other experts dismiss this figure and suggest that, with better management, the earth is capable of supporting its present numbers, and more. In fact, it is probably impossible to arrive at an ideal population level. This is partly because there is no agreement on what constitutes a reasonable standard of living. Also, we cannot predict how future technologies may affect the supply of global food and energy resources. However, a fairer distribution of resources would reduce at least some of the problems currently associated with overpopulation.

So what can we do?

The following measures may help to address the challenge of overpopulation:

- All the evidence suggests that economic development is the most effective way to tackle overpopulation. Rich nations should encourage poorer countries to develop in a sustainable way, so that they do not destroy their own resources, particularly forests.

■ Improvements to infrastructure, including transport links, communications, schools, hospitals and energy could reduce the impact of large populations on resources. Rich countries could help poorer nations make these improvements.

■ Many developing countries need to expand education, health care and social services. The evidence suggests that better health and education encourages people to plan their families and have fewer children.

■ Richer nations can support the development of alternative, more sustainable, industries and renewable resources. They can also encourage their populations to use fewer of the world's resources by conserving energy and recycling.

■ Governments could offer financial incentives, such as tax reductions or increased state benefits, to encourage people to have smaller families.

A young AIDS orphan, Chazile Mamba, receives help at a primary school in Swaziland, Southern Africa. Her schooling is funded through the state by the Global Fund, a coalition of governments, businesses and charities. Help such as this is essential in improving people's prospects and may ultimately lead to a less overcrowded world.

AT THE CROSSROADS

Niger is a large country in West Africa, plagued by droughts and threatened by the expanding Sahara Desert. It has a population of 14 million and a population growth rate of nearly three per cent. It has the highest fertility rate (7.2 births per woman) but also the highest child mortality rate (248 per 1000 before the age of four) in the world. Its economy is based largely on subsistence agriculture. Niger stands at a crossroads. It has recently introduced a Poverty Reduction Strategy Plan that focuses on improving health and primary education, reforming agriculture through land agreements (allowing greater access to land by local people), reducing corruption and conserving the environment. The international banks to which Niger owes money have reduced its debt, freeing up to US$40 million per year to help fund these developments. Perhaps Niger is on the brink of its own demographic transition.

Overpopulation is a complicated issue. Poverty, insecurity and lack of opportunity are some of the factors that encourage people to have large families. Better living conditions, education and security have the opposite effect. Improving the quality of life for people worldwide may be the most effective way to solve our growing population problem. It certainly wouldn't hurt.

DEBATE

You are in charge

You are the representative of a developed country at a meeting to discuss the problem of global overpopulation. A representative of another developed country makes a strong statement, saying that poorer countries need to begin implementing drastic measures to address their population numbers; this should include actively encouraging couples to have fewer children, including financial penalties for people having large families.

- You support the idea, pointing out that China has successfully reduced its population growth rate to below 2 children per couple by targeting family size directly. You recognize there are problems with this approach but say that any other measures will simply be too slow to take effect.

- You suggest that rich nations help poorer countries to develop more rapidly, encouraging the demographic transition. You recognize this will take longer but think it a more humane solution in the long term.

Glossary

age profile The analysis, by age, of a country or region's population. Poorer countries often have an age profile dominated by children and young people; richer countries have a more regular age profile, including large numbers of older people.

billion A thousand million.

birth control Methods by which couples avoid having children as a way of planning the size of their families.

consumption How much, or many, resources we use up, or consume.

demographic transition The change in population structure and size that normally occurs when a country or region undergoes development.

desalination The process of removing salt from seawater to produce drinking water.

desertification A process by which land becomes increasingly dry until almost no vegetation can grow on it.

developed world Richer regions such as North America, Japan and most of Europe, which have highly developed industries, infrastructure and technological capabilities.

developing world Poorer parts of the world, such as parts of Africa and South-East Asia, which are still largely based on a rural and agricultural economy.

drought A long period of very dry weather when there is not enough rain to grow crops successfully or replenish water supplies.

fertility rate The average number of children born to women who live beyond their childbearing years.

fossil fuels Fuels derived from coal, oil or gas (i.e. the fossilized remains of prehistoric plants and animals). Burning these fuels releases carbon dioxide into the atmosphere.

genetic To do with genes, which are the basic units within plants and animals that are capable of transmitting characteristics from one generation to the next.

genetic engineering The alteration of the genetic material of a plant or animal to create particular desired characteristics, such as rapid growth or resistance to disease.

global warming The increase in the average temperature of the earth's surface, caused in part by the build-up of greenhouse gases in the atmosphere.

infrastructure The large-scale public systems, services and facilities of a country, including public transportation, power and water supplies, telecommunications, roads, schools and hospitals.

life expectancy The average expected lifespan of an individual born in a particular country or region.

malnutrition A lack of healthy foods in a diet, leading to physical harm.

property rights The right of people to own, or have access to, land to support themselves and their families.

replacement rate The fertility rate at which the number of people being born in a population equals and replaces the number of people dying, so that the population growth rate is zero. Most experts agree that the replacement rate is about 2.1.

salinization A process by which surface soils dry out, causing salty water from deep in the water table to be drawn to the surface, making the land unsuitable for farming.

sustainable development Economic development that preserves resources for future generations.

tax revenue The income a government receives through taxation (the money it charges its citizens), which it then uses to run the government and the country.

unsustainable development Economic development that uses up resources, such as oil and water, until they are gone.

World Heritage Sites Protected ecological and historical sites and areas, recognized for their uniqueness and international importance.

Further Information

Books

Africa: Progress and Problems: Population and Overcrowding by Tunde Obadina (Mason Crest Publishers, 2007)

Earth's Changing Landscape: Population Growth by Philip Steele (Franklin Watts, 2004)

If the World Were a Village by David Smith and Shelagh Armstrong (A&C Black, 2003)

21st Century Debates: An Overcrowded World? by Rob Bowden (Wayland, 2002)

People on the Move: Economic Migrants by Dave Dalton (Heinemann Library, 2006)

Planet under Pressure: Population by Paul Mason (Raintree Publications, 2006)

Sustainable Future: World Population by Nance Lui Fyson (Franklin Watts, 2000)

Websites

www.eoearth.org
The website of the Encyclopedia of Earth. Click on population under 'topics'.

www.overpopulation.org
The website of World Population Awareness. It contains recent news and developments on the topic.

www.peopleandplanet.net
A useful gateway to global issues, including population.

www.un.org/esa/population//publications/wpp2006/WPP2006_Highlights_rev.pdf
The 2006 UN updated report on World Population Prospects. It contains a useful summary at the beginning.

en.wikipedia.org/wiki/world_population
Useful statistics and case studies.

Author's note: The books cited in the above list are generally neutral as regards population issues. However, some of the websites, while offering useful information, are not necessarily neutral and need to be viewed with caution.

Debate Panel answers

Page 5:

Do you give aid to a poor neighbouring country or encourage it to be more self-sufficient? You do not want the neighbouring country to become dependent on you and you certainly want to encourage it to become more self-sufficient. However, it may be more realistic in the short term to assist the country in improving its economy, so it will be less dependent in the future. For this reason, it may be wise to include agreements in which the neighbouring country undertakes to introduce measures to reduce its population growth. You may want to consider what these might be.

Page 11:

What sort of information would you require to help you predict the population growth of a developing country? Birth and death rates are clearly important factors in determining population growth, but they do not tell the whole story. Life expectancy also affects population size. Equally important, however, are what may be called social factors. Education (not only primary) is one of these, since levels of education often affect people's decisions on family size. Other important indicators include the level of health care, employment opportunities and the ability of the society to look after its old people.

Page 17:

Should you implement land reforms in your developing country even though a drought is looming? You need to decide what is in the best interests of your country and your people. This may mean putting back the reforms to avert an immediate crisis and concentrating your efforts on short-term measures such as improved storage facilities. You will need to convince your critics, however, that this is not a delaying tactic and offer them evidence that you are genuine about introducing the land reforms that you promised in your election campaign!

Page 31:

Battling illegal immigration isn't easy. People have proposed building fences and increasing border patrols, but it's impossible to completely seal off a country. Rounding up all illegal immigrants is equally impossible, short of doing a house-to-house search, which wouldn't be practical or popular. Some people argue that ejecting all illegal immigrants from a country would leave a big hole in the workforce.

Giving illegal workers legal status could solve some problems associated with illegal immigrants by helping them become contributing members of society. However, that could encourage more people to come illegally.

Page 39:

Do you try to speed up the demographic transition in your country through campaigns and incentives, or allow it to occur more slowly through longer term improvements? Perhaps the best solution in this case is not to look at these as alternatives – you could do both! In other words, you could have both a short- and long-term strategy. You could launch a media campaign and introduce financial incentives, but these will not be effective unless people can see the benefits of having smaller families. This requires better education, better health care, greater job security and many other improvements to people's lives. In India there is some evidence that living standards are beginning to rise rapidly, while the rate of population growth is falling.

Page 45:

Do you attempt to force drastic measures on poor countries to slow down their population growth or encourage rich countries to help their development? We cannot tell other countries what to do, but only encourage them to take certain courses of action. China's One-Child Policy was undoubtedly successful in achieving its immediate aim of reducing population growth, but led to other demographic problems that China is still dealing with. People may argue that they have the right to have as many children as they want, but this needs be balanced against the right of people everywhere to have enough food. Globally, however, development is the single most important factor in curbing population size. It is in all our interests that the rich nations of the world support this process in every way possible.

Index

Page numbers in **bold** refer to illustrations and charts.